A BEGINNER'S GUIDE TO EARLY PARENTING

A BEGINNER'S GUIDE TO EARLY PARENTING

Kunle & Bukky Akintayo

First published in 2019

ISBN 978-1-64570-695-3

Cover design: Fresh Design, Vancouver Island, Canada

Page design and production: Chapter One Book Production, Knebworth, UK

CONTENTS

DEDICATION

To our daughter, Tobi

To our partners at Culbeat Foundation

To God

We'd also like to thank our friend, Adanna Bankole, for proofreading the early drafts and manuscripts, Catherine Williams who guided us through the entire publishing experience and our editor, Alice Horne.

PREFACE

I grew up in Ado-Ekiti in the southwestern region of Nigeria but have lived in the United Kingdom for most of my married life. Southwest Nigeria has one of the highest child mortality rates in the world: The World Health Organization (WHO) estimates that, in Nigeria, 201 out of 1,000 children under 5 years (U5MR*) will die. I understand that Africa is poor, and sub-Saharan Africa even more so, but a 20% mortality rate is simply inexcusable. The unfortunate thing is that the mortality rate of mothers is almost as high as that of their children, but this goes largely unreported.

But don't think for a minute that this is a problem for the poor. There is a reason why many middle-to-upper-class Africans travel abroad to have their babies. While one key driver may be to have a good international passport, another is to avoid needless death and the dearth of ante- and postnatal services. In 2006, I lost a friend to complications arising from childbirth. She had waited almost a decade to marry her husband and had conceived within the first year of her marriage. She died on her hospital bed, leaving behind a husband and a daughter who are both scarred for life: a daughter who feels responsible for her mother's death, and a husband who could have afforded to send his wife abroad for proper care but chose to have the baby in Nigeria for the sake of patriotism.

I have always been concerned about this, and in 2010, I asked our team at the Culbeat Foundation – a charity that I founded with my wife – to begin the annual Day of Free Medical Consultation programme. It is a programme that focuses on providing education, free consultation, medication and advice to mothers and their new babies. We are lucky that the programme has now run for eight years and, despite mixed results, it must continue; there is still a huge amount of work to be done in this arena.

I thank our friends from the Nigerian Red Cross Society, MumsAloud and Casa Foundation who have supported this initiative over the last few years. This book is written in recognition of the work they do with us at Culbeat Foundation and in the hope that we will save many more mothers and children through good education.

Adekunle Akintayo
Doha, 2019

* U5MR is the under-five mortality ratio. This statistic differs from UNICEF and other organisations, but whichever source you refer to, the number is far too high in Nigeria.

LIST OF ILLUSTRATIONS

Part I:
BACKGROUND

CHAPTER 1

Introduction

Without an iota of doubt, being a parent is, in my opinion, the single largest responsibility that can be given to a human being. It comes down to having day-to-day charge of another human life until that dependent life is able, capable and indeed willing to assume that responsibility on their own. It transcends the responsibility given to national leaders or corporate executives in that the responsibility of a parent is direct, close and any successes (or failures) develop and evolve with the parent over time. National or corporate leaders can resign or retire; parents – at least responsible ones – are not afforded that opportunity.

I recall the film 'Nine months' in which the actor Hugh Grant plays a flashy, playboy-type character who is forced to make the adjustments most parents do as they welcome their babies into their homes and lives. In the film, Grant initially drives a two-seater Ferrari that fits perfectly into his carefree lifestyle, but it is incompatible with raising a baby: there is no space for a car seat. He soon realises that he must make changes to avoid losing his new family.

Parents have to make such decisions year on year: deferring their dreams of a bigger house, switching to a family-size car, postponing further study, choosing not to live in their preferred city or not working their dream job, all in order to raise their children.

Although many parents have made this choice – that is, to forego a dream in order to do the 'right and responsible' thing – many would-be parents do not have the faintest idea of how this should be done and have to rely on snippets from the internet, or even old wives' tales, to learn how to raise their children.

I fell into this latter category. Married at 32, I was interested in having a family but, try as we might, my wife and I had to wait for more than five years. When we finally conceived, I researched my network for some reliable information on what to expect, and I have to confess that there were few resources on how to raise a child. There were a few good books on pregnancy and what mothers need to be aware of, but there was certainly nothing of note for would-be fathers.

That is the raison d'être for this book. It is a 'beginner's guide' to the process of having and raising a child. Obviously, raising a human being is a huge subject over which no one can claim mastery. To this end, the scope of the book will be limited from late pregnancy to early childhood, covering the 'toddling' years from the ages of zero to three.

The book has been co-authored by my wife and me. I wrote most of the book from the perspective of a father who watched and supported my wife through a changing and testing time of our lives. My wife wrote the critical parts detailing a mother recovery after the birth of your baby and on the feedback from other mothers.

We chose to begin at the third trimester of pregnancy because, in our view, this is the latest point at which the real preparations must start until the child is three years old and they are ready to go to kindergarten (at least in most countries).

Having established the scope, I will quickly mention the big elephant in the room: culture. Needless to say, the traditions and norms observed in raising children vary widely. There is no doubt that having myself been raised in rural Nigeria, where raising a child is more of a communal effort, my upbringing was very different from how I have raised my daughter in a suburb just outside London, England.

The significance of culture in raising a child cannot be overstated. For me, it is the sole most important factor in whether a child can be raised successfully or not. However, this topic is again too broad to be covered in one book. Instead, this book will consider parenting from a general, cosmopolitan view with a generic bias to parents living in cities.

Some issues covered in this book are practical, for example how to set up a child's room or choose their clothing, but the book also includes factual advice on topics such as the mandatory vaccinations and inoculations a child must have and at what stages these must occur.

We believe such a book is essential – even mandatory – today for two reasons. Firstly, globalisation means that many Generation X parents and millennials are travelling farther from 'home' and therefore have reduced access to the family networks and support that generations before them enjoyed at the critical points of childbirth and in early child development. Secondly, as the baby-boomer generation reaches its sunset years, younger generations have fewer sources of information on childcare, and an established body of knowledge can only be preserved through proper documentation such as ante this book.

We hope that this book is a blessing to you and that you recommend it to others. Happy early parenting!

Part II
PREGNANCY AND BIRTH

CHAPTER 2

Antenatal Care

In many ways, I was not really the ideal parenting partner. I often forgot the scan appointments, and when I remembered, I would be at work. I recall going to an antenatal class with my wife where we sat in a circle like in an AA meeting, opening up to complete strangers. Given that I come from a fairly conservative background, this first meeting felt very strange! But I grew into it and in fact actively participated as time went on. In this section, I will cover the key issues relating to late pregnancy and antenatal care.

2.1: The trimesters

For me, the real preparation started during the third trimester of the pregnancy; it is best, however, that both partners are involved from the point of conception. A typical pregnancy lasts for 40 weeks from the date of the last menstrual cycle until the birth of a child. This 40-week period is divided into three trimesters. The first trimester is usually seen as lasting from conception to 12 weeks. This period is considered by some medical professionals as the most critical in the baby's development since this is when all the major internal organs are formed. The second trimester runs from week 13 to 28, and in this time, the baby's musculoskeletal systems should start to form, and it should move, hear and develop other functional systems. The third trimester, from week 29 to 40, is when the kicking and contractions begin. You can also expect your wife to visit the toilet so often that both of you become embarrassed. Note that, by week 37, the baby is considered to have come to full term and its organs should be capable of functioning on their own.

Tip: A good resource for finding out what happens from week to week is available via the NHS website https://www.nhs.uk/conditions/pregnancy-and-baby/

2.2: What's a scan?

Both mother and child will experience significant changes during each of the trimesters. There are several good books and websites that provide more detailed information on what to expect. In the third trimester, couples will need to attend a number of ultra-sound scanning sessions to observe the development of the baby.

In the United Kingdom for example, mothers are expected to attend at least two ultrasound scans as follows:

Week	Purpose
Weeks 8–14	Ultrasound 'dating' scan to check physical development and whether the mother is expecting more than one baby. The scan could also be used screen for abnormalities, such as Down's syndrome although this is not mandatory
Weeks 18–21	Anomaly scan to check that there are no physical abnormalities

There is more to ultrasound scanning than simply photographing the foetus. Hospitals use scans as an opportunity to monitor the baby's development and to screen mothers for transferrable diseases such as HIV/AIDS, hepatitis B/C and syphilis, among others.

So what really happens during the scan? When we had ours, my wife was invited in to check her vitals, was asked to change into a hospital gown and to sit in a chair like those you find at the dentist and to open her legs. A cold jelly was applied to her stomach and a ball, rather like a computer mouse, was rolled over it to get pictures of the baby.

And guess what? After all that excitement, the baby could be asleep! There was one instance when we went for the scan and the doctor could not perform the necessary checks for that precise reason. We were advised to walk up and down the stairs of the five or so floors of the hospital to wake her up.

I cannot overemphasise the need to attend these scans, particularly if you feel that something could be amiss. In some cases, babies cease to respond, which can indicate a foetal death or missed abortion. I am familiar with a case where the baby's heartbeat was unheard during a scheduled scan and, in another case, there was a lack of movement, both pointing to a foetal death. It is always best to consult your doctor in such cases, as spontaneous abortion could occur or a dilation and curettage (D&C) procedure could be required.

That said, in most cases, there is nothing to worry about except for your baby taking a nap.

Tip: The scanning process can be a bit invasive and women should request a female nurse beforehand, if they prefer.

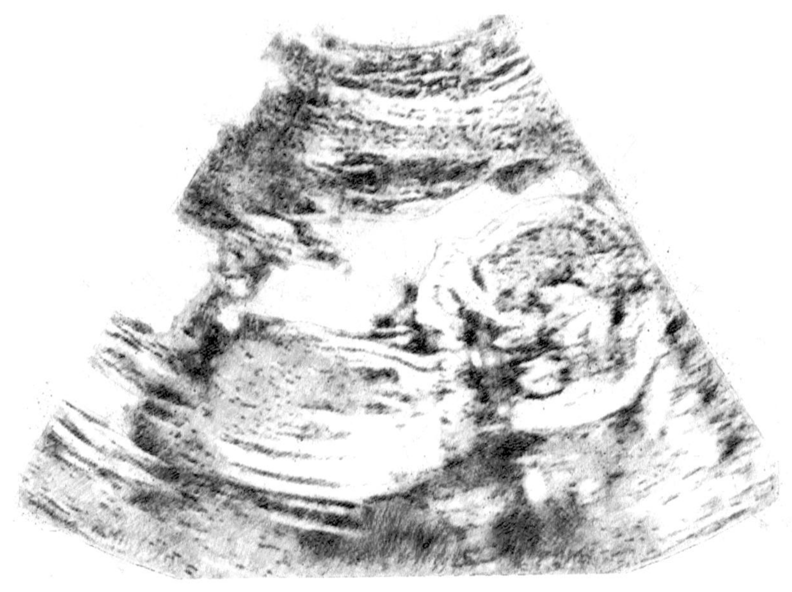

Figure 2-1: Ultrasound scan of a baby

2.3: Antenatal classes

The whole purpose of antenatal classes is to prepare parents for the birth process and early parenthood. It is strongly recommended that both parents attend when possible, particularly for first-time parents. I attended three of these classes with my wife at different stages of her pregnancy. Depending on the country, antenatal care is organised by the hospital where the mother-to-be is registered or by an independent local council. From my experience, these classes are run by midwives, nurses and/or mothers.

The subjects taught in the classes may also vary from place to place, but it is likely that soon-to-be parents will be taught about topics including food, rest, breathing exercises, birth positions, birth methods, vaccinations and support available from hospitals and local councils.

Tip: You'll need to decide where and how you'd like the birth of your baby to take place early so that your antenatal care can be tailored to your chosen method. There is no point learning about hospital birthing methods if you are going to deliver the baby at home! Seek information on what options are available.

The most interesting antenatal classes for me happened in week 36 or so, about two weeks before our baby was due. The session leader emphasised the need for fathers to be particularly considerate during these final stages with the following key pieces of advice:

- Be as supportive as possible
- Give up the remote control. Your wife could probably do with less football or cricket at this point!

Tip: Fathers, make sure that you go to antenatal classes with your partner. Some of the activities and exercises can be a bit embarrassing if only one parent-to-be attends the class! Imagine a class of 10 couples where only your partner is alone.

2.4: Birth methods

For me, antenatal classes highlighted lots of new information. I had always known that women either had Caesarean sections or gave birth naturally, but I was surprised by just how advanced both methods had become, as well as the other options now available.

If you opt for the Caesarean section, you must come to a decision on time so that the hospital is prepared. My wife – who chose to have a

Caesarean section – speaks very highly of the epidural injection given to women prior to the operation to numb the pain. These injections are delivered by a specialist who may not be available at all hospitals, so be sure to check this well in advance.

In some countries, fathers can be present during the birth, but other cultures may frown on this. In the United Kingdom, fathers are allowed into the theatre alongside a few medical personnel who support the surgeon with the delivery. The process itself is rather quick; I was in the theatre for less than 40 minutes. The mother is sedated with an anaesthetic, the Caesarean section is performed, the baby is given to the father and then quickly withdrawn for the initial care and vital checks. If all goes well, the mother could be back in her ward in a couple of hours, including a post-surgery rest period.

On the other hand, I learnt that the natural birthing process has evolved over the last decade or so. These days, parents-to-be can choose from a variety of methods, including the use of birth pools and warm pools. The use of gas and air is now standard in most hospitals, as is TENS (transcutaneous electrical nerve stimulation), a pulse-inducing transmitter that is connected to the body and sends pulses to the brain to prevent pain signals from reaching it. (This might sound complicated, but it is similar to the ECG machines found in most hospitals.)

In our case, we were shown to a clean room and had a midwife attending to us. She periodically checked my wife's dilation on a scale of one to ten. It is normal for most women to have the help of a midwife right through the birth, but if complications occur, a doctor will be brought in. For us, the midwife noticed that my wife was not dilating well. After several 'pushes', the baby had become stressed, and we were immediately moved to the theatre. You cannot underestimate the need for a good doctor at this point. Other complications could involve the baby being breech (lying bottom or feet first) or premature. If labour starts before the completion of the third trimester, it is best to opt for a hospital birth.

Tip: It is a good idea to visit the hospital before the due date to familiarise yourself with access, parking and other important details. You don't want to be looking for the right entrance on the day when you are already under a lot of pressure!

2.5: Post birth and getting ready to go home

Congratulations! You have just had your baby and this is likely to be one of the proudest moments of your life. However, such great pride comes with great responsibilities.

Depending on the ease of the birth, parents may be allowed to return home after a few hours or may have to remain in the postnatal ward for more observation. After my wife's Caesarean section, we stayed in a rest area for about three hours and were then transferred to the general ward. We stayed in the hospital for three days before we were discharged.

Visiting rules will vary from hospital to hospital. The matrons and nurses in the postnatal ward will let you know the visiting hours and other rules, such as rest and feeding times for mother and baby. Before leaving the hospital, make sure the necessary forms are completed to avoid future complications. It is not unusual for the hospital to perform some preliminary tests, such as auditory and sight tests.

In our case, our daughter did not 'latch on', meaning she did not suck as well as expected. The paediatrician rubbed a little sweet syrup on her gum to simulate the sucking, and the problem was solved. Mother and child were given an additional day to rest and for further observations, then it was time for us to go home to start our new life!

Part III

BRINGING YOUR BABY HOME

CHAPTER 3

Setting Up for the Baby

3.1: Parenting support aids

Can you guess the average tonnage of equipment that you will need to buy for a new baby? To help you guess, these are just some of the items you may want to buy:

- Cot and mattress
- Moses basket
- Baby indoor seat (bouncy seat)
- Baby bath station or changing table
- Stroller or walker
- Car seat (in the European Union, you cannot even drive home without one of these!)
- Baby harness
- High chair
- Clothing
- Nappies
- Wardrobe
- Bath tub
- Toys
- Feeding bottles
- Breast-feeding pillows

In my estimation, you will acquire around 200kg of equipment to cater for a 4–6kg baby!

We had bought some of the items on this list, but the most important gift we received was the baby changing station where we could give our daughter her daily bath with minimum fuss. If you can, I strongly recommend that you set up a room at home with the cot

Figure 3-1: A baby changing station

and baby station, which should hold all the materials that you need to provide daily care for your baby. The experts will say that the room should be bright and airy; I will just suggest that you make it as practical as possible for the mother or whoever is responsible for providing the child's primary care.

Tip: Never underestimate the challenge involved in giving a baby a bath! I strongly recommend the use of a baby changing station, a table-like apparatus with a bath tub and a built-in cabinet which can hold your baby's bathing and changing equipment.

Many parents choose a colour theme for their baby's room depending on whether they are having a boy or a girl, and choose matching bedsheets, pillows and other accessories. However, the most important thing is that the room is clean, tidy and kept at an appropriate temperature. Cleanliness is of critical importance because the baby has a low level of immunity. To prevent germs and infections from spreading, you might want to have a washbasin close by or at least hand sanitiser for visitors who may hold the baby.

3.2: Clothing

I will not even attempt to define the clothing requirements for a baby. Certainly, the clothing requirements will vary significantly between Europe and Africa. The key here is to be sensible and to keep your baby at the right temperature.

Tip: Wherever you are, it is recommended that your baby wears a cap to keep its head warm. You should also avoid loose items of clothing or clothes with straps to avoid the risk of choking.

We had our daughter at the beginning of November, just at the onset of winter, and this helped us decide what clothing she needed. Whatever you choose, you cannot go wrong with a few one-piece suits, sleepers and some leggings.

We were given a few rules about dressing appropriately for the weather, but if the temperature is less than -6°C (21°F), stay indoors. Indoor temperatures should be in the range of 18–21°C (64–70°F).

	Situation	Clothing
Indoors	Normal temperature	Sleep suit and one-piece suit
	House is cold	As above, but with a jumper
	Baby is sweating or has flushed cheeks	Remove one layer
Outdoors	Warm temperature	Light clothing, plus a jumper
	Cold temperature	Sleep suit, one-piece suit and snowsuit or fleece

Whatever you do, you can be sure that your baby will let you know if they are not comfortable! Keep checking for any signs of discomfort and be sure to respond promptly.

3.3: Feeding your baby

Many parents, particularly first-time parents, find feeding their baby an area of concern. Your questions start right at the hospital: how can you make sure your baby gets the nourishment they need? What do you do if they refuse to latch onto the mother? Suppose the mother becomes indisposed after birth, or perhaps she is unable to lactate? Should any of these situations arise, it is best to contact your midwife or paediatrician for advice.

Nutrition in your baby's first year is especially important because experience and interaction with other parents, it seems that most babies or toddlers are less selective thereafter. Feeding in the first year is done in three ways:

- Exclusive breast-feeding
- Bottle-feeding
- Mix of breast and bottle-feeding

An increasing number of mothers opt for exclusive breast-feeding, as is often encouraged by health workers. It is said that a mother's very first milk after birth, called colostrum, is a natural and safe vaccine containing large quantities of an antibody called secretory immunoglobulin A (SIgA), which protects newborn babies against diseases. After this, breast milk provides all the nutrients that the child needs to survive and develop, so it is easy to see why breast-feeding comes highly recommended.

The downside to exclusive breast-feeding – which becomes apparent after a few months as your baby begins to grow – is that they will need more food and so more frequent feeding. Just after birth, it is normal to nurse the baby whenever they are hungry, which is typically between every one-and-a-half to three hours. As a guideline, therefore, babies can be expected to nurse between seven and 10 times a day, drinking 45–90ml of milk each time, for the first two months of life. From month three, they could be drinking 120ml every three to four hours.

Mothers are very likely to experience breast milk secretion even when the baby is not feeding, so to maintain hygiene, it is recommended that the nipple areas are rinsed before feeding. Another recommendation is to use breast pads as these can absorb the secretion and protect the mother's modesty.

On occasion, mothers may need to feed the baby in awkward positions. For example, it is not uncommon for babies to continue to breast-feed as they fall asleep, and it can become difficult to support the weight of the baby in these positions without disturbing them. In these situations, breast-feeding pillows can be very helpful. These pillows are not a 'must-have', but they are certainly worth investigating.

The recommendation from most health workers is to breast-feed the baby for at least a year, though this may be difficult in practical terms. I would advise a minimum of six months of breast-feeding in view of the enormous long-term benefits for both mother and baby.

For working mothers, this can be even more of a challenge. Sadly, we can't all live in Norway and benefit from their generous 12 months of paid parental leave! So, if you are returning to work after three months or so, a breast pump will come in handy. This is a device that nursing mothers use to extract milk from their breasts. It will come with bottles of various sizes which can be attached to the pump to store the extracted milk. This milk can then be fed to your baby from the bottle when the mother is unable to breast-feed directly.

Tip: The baby will need to be fed from alternate breasts. It is usually recommended to switch breasts every 10 minutes, otherwise milk in one breast is depleted whereas the other breast remains full, leaky and heavy, which can cause discomfort to the mother.

It takes a brave woman to breast-feed exclusively! In fact, it is normal to introduce the baby to bottle-feeding at some point within their first year. Processed baby milk products are categorised according to the age of the baby, and most will include instructions for how to make a bottle. Baby milk brands vary from country to country, but some of the popular baby milk brands in the United Kingdom include Aptamil® which holds over 50% of the market share, Cow & Gate (31% market share) and SMA (14%). Other popular brands across the globe include NAN, Similac, Enfamil and Mamia.

Figure 3-2:

Milks, purées and veggies

About the same time (or sometimes earlier), parents can introduce the baby to purées or puréed foods. These contain blended, mashed or crushed fruits or vegetables which can either be bought as branded off-the-shelf products or prepared at home. Some popular brands in the United Kingdom include Cow & Gate, Organix and Heinz. Purées provide good nutrition for babies as the fruit and vegetables can fulfil their dietary needs or supplement the nutrients they get from milk. Other useful supplements are porridges and baby rices such as CERELAC® or NUTRIENT®. These can be given to babies from the age of four months and are some of the best products available on the market for weaning babies from their milk diet.

3.4: About the bottle

A new parent might be surprised to find that a lot of fuss is made about baby bottles: the size of the bottle, the size of the teat on the bottle, how to sterilise the bottle and so on. Take the size of the bottle, for example. We originally bought large bottles because we thought that, as our baby grew and ate more, larger bottles would come in handy. The downside to this was food wastage and the recycling of unfinished milk. As you might expect, there are potential health issues with recycling milk products, particularly in tropical climates.

Feeding bottles come in three standard sizes: 4oz (about 120ml), 8oz (240ml) and 12oz (360ml). The 4oz bottle is popular because it holds the amount of milk that can be consumed in a single feeding session, which avoids the wastage associated with larger bottles. Bottle size should only be increased to match the baby's appetite as they grow.

The teat on the bottle is also sized or shaped to match the baby's age and feeding habits. Generally, a baby starts with a slow-feeding (smaller) teat and graduates to a faster-feeding (larger) teat as they grow. For babies that are three months and older, a flat teat with a slot is recommended, while for babies aged six months and above, it is best to use a teat with four holes as this helps the milk flow faster. Philips' AVENT baby range, which includes the latter kind of teat, is popular in this market. Whatever teats you use, they should be replaced every three months due to wear and tear.

Tip: Always choose anti-colic teats. These aim to reduce the amount of air your baby takes in while feeding, which helps to prevent colic. Colic is severe pain in the abdomen caused by wind or an obstruction in the intestines and the colon's muscular contractions as it attempts to remove it. It may be accompanied by vomiting and sweating.

Bottles, teats and anything else your baby uses for feeding should be washed and sterilised after each use. This is important because your

Figure 3-3: Feeding bottles and steriliser

baby's immune system is weaker than an adult's, so they are more susceptible to infections leading to vomiting, diarrhoea, oral thrush and so on. Sterilisation kills any germs in or on bottles or feeding utensils and can be done in a microwave, by steaming, boiling, using UV light or using chemicals (such as chlorine tablets) dissolved in water. We had an AVENT steriliser, which was very easy to use.

It is generally advised to sterilise your baby's utensils until they are 12 months old. You should also have a separate, dedicated brush or sponge to clean your baby's feeding items and avoid washing them in the dishwasher.

3.5: Postnatal visits

There is a local adage in southwestern Nigeria that the arrival of a child is accompanied with joy, dancing and celebrations. Nothing epitomises this better than the sheer number of visits that a new mother and baby can expect. Indeed, one of my main takeaways from postnatal classes was the need to manage visits from friends and family so that mother and baby can get adequate rest.

Tip: One way to limit visits is to set a visiting 'curfew', say between 7 and 8pm, every evening. This also gives you a good opportunity to prepare the baby for bed.

You have probably heard the saying 'I slept like a baby'. Well for most parents, it's not that simple. It's not unusual for babies to wake up as many as five times during the night to feed or as a result of some discomfort, and when the baby is awake, someone will need to check on them. You might think you'll have a chance to rest while the baby is asleep during the day, but you'll likely find that this is an opportune time to catch up with household chores instead. One approach we found useful was for my wife to go to bed early at night so she could get some much-needed rest before the expected interruptions would begin. Note that not all babies will wake consistently during the night, but it does seem to be the case for most.

One visit to schedule meticulously, however, is that of the midwife. In the United Kingdom, midwives are scheduled to visit the mother and the baby at least twice in the first few weeks after birth. Typically, a midwife will visit between five to seven days after to check if the clip from the umbilical cord is kept clean and if it is ready to fall off, the midwife will also use this opportunity to check the mother's health and general recovery. This is particularly important if birth was by Caeserean section as the midwife will review the post-surgery healing process.

The second visit of the midwife follows within a week of the first, and during this visit, the midwife weighs the baby and performs a blood test. I recall the second visit vividly. The blood test (sometimes called the heel prick test in the United Kingdom) involves collecting a sample of blood from the baby's heel by piercing it with a sharp, flat blade. Seeing this blade and how my daughter's heel was squeezed in order to obtain the blood sample, I was livid! Fortunately, my wife took the episode much better than I did, but if you would rather not see your baby bleed, it may be better to excuse yourself.

Once the midwife visits are concluded, the mother and newborn may be handed into the care of a health visitor. The health visitor is responsible for scheduling the baby's hearing test and immunisations. These appointments are logged in a medical record book issued to all newborn babies in the United Kingdom to detail their progress from birth to the age of five years. The book is often referred to as the NHS 'red book' in the United Kingdom. Details of the red book are provided in Section 3.6. Similar record books exist in other countries, for example in South Korea.

It goes without saying that the timings for these scheduled visits vary from country to country. The point to remember is that certain activities have to be performed after birth to ensure that the newborn is in the best health and that any medical issues are flagged early so that the baby can obtain the appropriate treatment.

Here are some of the tests our daughter undertook and their approximate timings.

Test	Timing (approx.)	Location
Paediatrician assessment	Within 72 hours	Hospital
Initial hearing and sight test	Within 72 hours	Hospital
Weighing	Within 10–14 days	Home
Heel prick test	Within 10–14 days	Home
Full medical examination	6–8 weeks after birth	Hospital
First immunisation	8 weeks after birth	Hospital

3.6: Immunisation schedule

A child's personal health record (or the NHS red book in the United Kingdom) is used to document their health and development. This book is used in some form in most countries.

Broadly, the book is divided into four sections and holds the following information for a child from birth to early childhood:

- Section 1: baby's details, family details, local resources (such as GP practices and hospitals) and information relevant to the care of the newborn
- Section 2: immunisations, vaccinations and jabs. Details of all such vaccinations are recorded in the book and can be made available to health and school authorities on demand
- Section 3: records of visits from the midwife and health visitor and the results of tests including the hearing and eye tests
- Section 4: information and measurements relating to the baby's growth, including comparison with local averages and percentiles

As mentioned above, one main purpose of the health book is to record a history of the child's immunisations. Babies are generally immunised against the following diseases (source: Made for Mums):

- Pneumococcal infection (a bacterial infection causing meningitis, septicaemia and pneumonia)
- Diphtheria (an infectious disease affecting the lungs and causing mild fever)
- Tetanus (toxins in the blood from open wounds)
- Pertussis or whooping cough (a bacterial infection that clogs the lungs with mucus)
- Polio (a viral infection of the central nervous system)
- Hepatitis B (an infection of the liver

- Meningitis (inflammation of the meninges, caused by viral or bacterial infection)
- Measles (a childhood viral infectious often evidenced by fever and a red rash)
- Mumps (a contagious and infectious viral disease, causing swelling of the parotid salivary glands)
- Rubella or German measles (a contagious viral disease, with symptoms like mild measles)

The schedule for immunisations is as follows:

Timing after birth	Vaccination	Purpose
Week 8	DTaP/IPV/Hib/HepB	A six-in-one jab protecting against diphtheria, tetanus, pertussis, polio, Haemophilus influenzae type B (Hib) and hepatitis B
	PCV	Protects against pneumococcal infection
Week 12	DTaP/IPV/Hib/HepB	Second DTaP/IPV/Hib/HepB jab
	Men C	Protects against meningitis C
Week 16	DTaP/IPV/Hib/HepB	Third DTaP/IPV/Hib/HepB jab
	PCV	Second PCV jab
	Men C	Second meningitis C jab
Month 12	Hib	Fourth Hib jab
	Men C	Third meningitis C jab
Month 13	MMR	Three-in-one jab for mumps, measles and rubella
	PCV	Third PCV jab

PRIMARY COURSE OF IMMUNISATION

please press firmly

Please place a sticker (if available) otherwise write in space provided.

Surname

First names

NHS Number Sex M / F

Address

Post Code D.O.B

G.P. Code

H.V. Code

Breastfeeding

at 1st Imm:
Totally ☐ Partially ☐ Not at all ☐

at 2nd Imm:
Totally ☐ Partially ☐ Not at all ☐

at 3rd Imm:
Totally ☐ Partially ☐ Not at all ☐

Antigen	Date	Batch No	Site	Signature	Immuniser Name in CAPITALS	Venue
DTaP/IPV/Hib						
PVC						
DTaP/IPV/Hib						
MEN C						
DTaP/IPV/Hib						
MEN C						
PVC						

Figure 3-4: Immunisation page from the NHS red book

CHAPTER 4

The Equipment

This section will cover the main pieces of equipment that parents rely on during the early developmental phase of a baby's growth. New parents will find themselves with a huge checklist of essentials, and it is not our intention to cover every item here. Moreover, the necessary equipment varies from one culture to another. The list that we have focused on in this section may be more associated with Western cultures, but other cultures will have similar equipment for the same purposes.

One equipment that is conspicuously absent in the section is the baby changing station since it is discussed in some detail in section 3.1. As I mentioned previously, this is the most important piece of equipment that we received or bought for tending to our baby's needs.

4.1: Moses basket

Taking its name from the biblical character Moses and the basket of reeds used to hide him from a murderous Pharaoh, this is essentially a portable bed which is large enough for your baby, but small enough to tuck away neatly in a corner of your living room.

Although the Moses basket provides a comfortable place for the baby to sleep, it is different from the cot, which is larger and normally kept in the baby or parents' bedroom. Unlike a cot, the Moses basket is often placed in the living area and is used during the day so that parents and visitors can have easy access to the baby. Some baskets come with a rocking stand which can help the baby get to sleep.

From my experience, most babies do not sleep in the Moses basket for long, and even when already asleep, a baby placed in a basket tends to wake up shortly afterwards. This suggests to me that they may not be as comfortable as they look in brochures! Nonetheless, they serve the purpose of providing easy access during the daytime and are still a recommended buy.

Figure 4-1:

A typical Moses basket

4.2: Seater/rocker

A seater is a sort of easy chair where a baby can recline and observe their surroundings. Many seaters are able to rock, come with an array of toys and rattles and some even have calming vibration settings. It is no surprise that babies tend to like their rockers a lot more than they like their Moses baskets.

Figure 4-2: A typical seater/rocker

The seater is also designed to support the baby's back better than when they are being carried. The only downside is that – as with everything else – they will quickly outgrow it. A seater's shelf life is limited to six months at best, but it is still a purchase we would recommend.

4.3: Walker

A baby walker helps a baby learn how to walk. Walkers have been around for centuries in various forms, but there are two common types today. With the first type, the baby can simply hold onto it and push it around. The second type allows a baby to stand and sit intermittently as they attempt to walk, making it better suited to younger or less adventurous babies, refer to figure 6.2 in section 6.6.

Figure 4-3: A typical baby walker

Tip: Babies can fall and hurt themselves using this kind of walker, so adequate attention and close monitoring should be given to the baby while it's in use.

For our daughter, we used a stationary baby play station instead of a walker. This helped her stand and strengthen her limbs while reducing the risk of her falling.

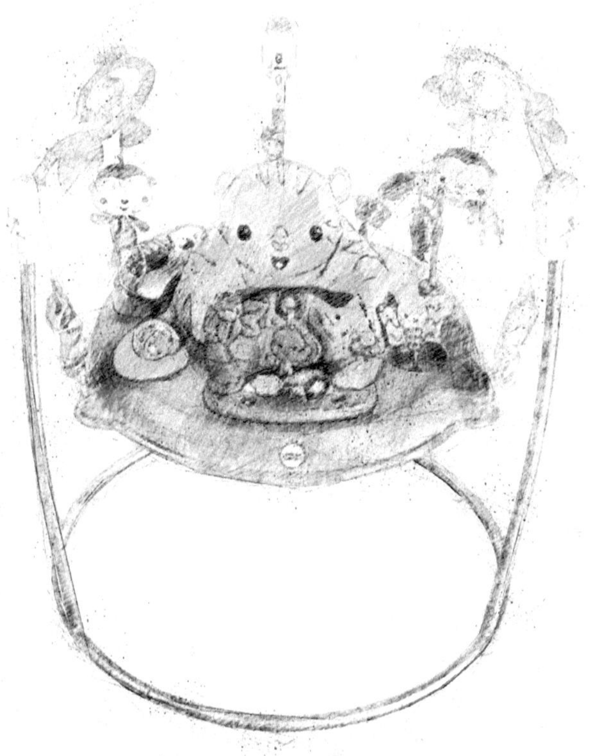

Figure 4-4: A typical baby play station

4.4: Car seat and mirror

Also known as a baby safety seat, a car seat is designed to protect a baby from injury in a car, or worse, in the event of an accident. In many countries today, the use of a car seat is required by law, and different categories of car seat are specified for children (including babies) depending on their age, weight and height.

In the United Kingdom, a mother and baby cannot even be discharged from hospital without the appropriate car seat, and car seats are required for children until they are 135cm tall or reach the age of 12. In other jurisdictions, such as the United States and Australia, regulations forbid the use of rear-facing baby seats in the front of vehicles, while Scandinavian countries expect children to sit in rear-facing seats until they are four years old.

Tip: For very young children, rear-facing seats are recommended until at least the age of one because they provide more support for the head. You may want to install a mirror on the centre back seat so that you can check on them easily.

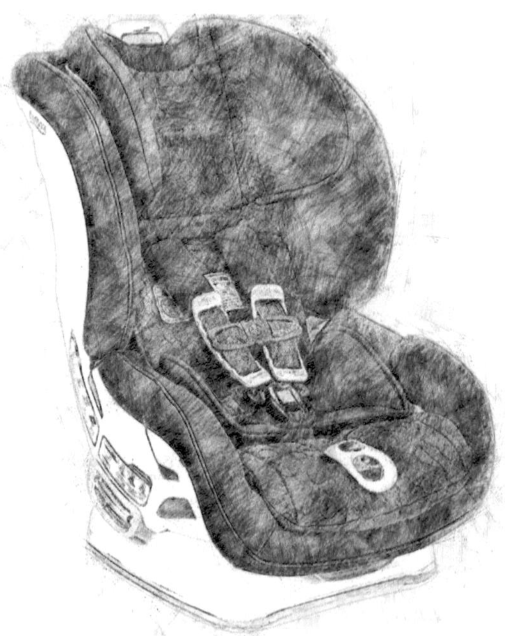

Figure 4-5:

A typical car seat

The International Organization for Standardization (ISO) has attempted to standardise and simplify the use of car seats. A summary of the car seat grouping according to European Union regulation R44/04 is shown below. There are more details about car seats and how they should be used in different countries on the European Union's mobility and transport website.

Group	Example and main feature(s)	Fixation	Weight group	Age range	Facing	Comments
Group 0	Fastened carry-cot Infant carriers No base	ISOFIX and/or adult seat belts	Up to 9.1kg (20lbs)	Birth to 15 months	Rear-facing	Popularly called a 'bucket carrier' due to its handle, these car seats act as a cocoon for the baby in the event of impact
Group 0+	Convertible seats Separate base	Adult seat belts	13kg (29lbs)	Birth to 15 months	Rear-facing	A popular type, particularly useful because they can be converted from rear-facing to front-facing
Group 1	Seat with no carrying handle, designed to stay in the car, and usually with a five-point baby harness	Adult seat belts	9–18kg (20–40lbs)	9 months to 4 years	Rear- or forward-facing	Uncommon except in Scandinavian countries
Group 2	Like Group 1 above, but larger	Adult seat belts	15–25kg (33–55lbs)	4 to 6 years	Rear- or forward-facing	
Group 3	Booster seats Forward-facing restraints	Adult seat belts	22–36kg (49–79lbs)	4 to 10 years	Forward-facing	These are used with the child sitting upright. Their purpose is to lift the child to improve the fit of the seat belt

The challenge with any car seat is that they can be difficult to use, so read the manual carefully before setting them up. Another option is a pushchair or pram with a detachable car seat. These may be expensive, but can be very practical. Make sure you research your options thoroughly based on what is suitable for your baby, car and/or situation.

4.5: Pushchair/pram

Prams, also known as strollers, come in various guises. Used as early as the Victorian period, prams are now very sophisticated with models including travel systems, jogging strollers, traditional strollers, double or triple strollers and so on. They can also be adapted to suit the baby's age. For example, a baby-style (parent-facing) pram, which is often used for younger babies or infants, can be transformed into a front-facing, sitting stroller for a toddler. We used one of these for our daughter, the advantage being that we didn't need to buy a new pram as she got older. On the downside, though, the cost can range anywhere between £50 to several thousand pounds.

Tip: If you are on a tight budget, it may actually be cheaper to buy a pram for your baby and replace it with a stroller when they become a toddler.

4.6: High chair

There is no set time when you can expect your baby to begin feeding themselves. Parents who are 'braver' and can allow for the impending mess may want to let their baby try this as early as possible. For others, this is likely to happen between 18 months and two years. One item that we found particularly useful for our daughter's independence during meal times was the high chair. We fastened her securely in the chair and let her feed herself while we could enjoy our meal too.

We also found the chair useful when getting our daughter ready for nursery in the mornings. Her food could be prepared and served, then we could dash around the house getting ready for work while she fed herself. I would say this was the second most essential item that we bought or received after the baby station.

Take care to ensure the high chair is set up properly to stop the baby escaping. In particular, the buckle must be loose enough to allow them to move, but secure enough to ensure their safety. You also need to make sure you keep the high chair clean, as babies tend to pick up food straight from the tray.

Figure 4-6:

A typical high chair

4.7: Playmat

Rather than let your baby play on the bare floor or carpet, play mats are a fun and safe place for your baby to play. They are particularly useful when your baby is just learning to roll, sit or crawl, but it may not be needed for a long period of time. In line with its short lifespan, its cost is relatively low.

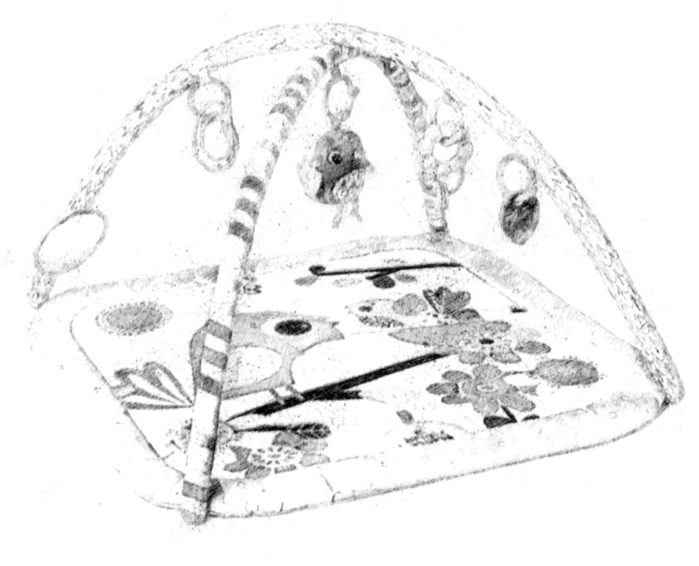

Figure 4-7: A typical play mat

4.8: Changing bag

For savvy parents, another important item is the baby's changing bag. For us, it was an absolute 'don't-leave-home-without-it' accessory.

Babies are babies, and unlike their parents, they pay no attention to the environment, timing or situation when it comes to nature's calls. You could be at a picnic, church service, visiting friends or in the middle of a career-changing interview when your baby chooses to relieve themselves.

There is no point getting embarrassed about this. The important thing is to be prepared, and that preparation is best demonstrated by packing a good baby changing bag. We bought one from Mothercare® for our daughter, and it was a life-saver. These days, changing bags are designed so fashionably that they can match your apparel seamlessly when you're out and about.

More importantly than making a fashion statement, though, a changing bag must contain everything your baby will need, such as:

- Changing mat
- Change of clothes
- Bibs
- Toy (at least one) or dummy
- Wipes
- Milk, food and snacks
- Nappies
- Nappy sack (plastic or biodegradable bags)
- Vaseline or powder
- Water
- Hand sanitiser

CHAPTER 5

Mum's Recovery

So far, who has been more concerned about the baby than the mother? You are in good company. Non-scientific polls suggest that this is a very common response among friends and family. However, research suggests that mothers need at least an equal – if not higher – level of attention after giving birth. This chapter is dedicated to understanding some of the key issues that mothers face and things to look out for. Bukola describes her personal recovery story in this section, as well as some general tips.

5.1: Our story

Each mother's recovery story is a unique experience, as every woman's body responds differently. I had a Caesarean section, so the initial recovery was expected to take longer, but I was up and about by day two, although I had a reaction to the anaesthetic given during surgery.

My body had expanded significantly over the nine-month period and required almost a year to return to its pre-birth size (assuming that it ever did!). As I had a Caesarean section, I was advised not to lift anything heavy and not to drive for six weeks to help my body recuperate faster.

Tip: Do not lift anything heavier than your baby during the first six weeks after childbirth, or until you have fully recovered from the birth.

Taking care of a newborn who feeds every two to four hours was very overwhelming for me, though the frequency of feeding does depend on the method you opt for. I also felt sad at times and was very emotional due to the lack of quality rest amidst all the visits from friends and loved ones. These visits made me feel obligated to do things rather than rest, and I would advise new mothers to be aware of this and to manage their time wisely. With some of my friends, I found it worked well to have a nap while they were visiting, leaving them to chat with my husband or my parents. I must emphasise, however, that such visits are necessary: imagine how you would feel if no one came to see you after childbirth!

A tough part of the day was when everyone had left for work, leaving me at home alone with the baby. My daughter would sleep for quite a while, but I wasn't able to use that time much given that she might wake up and need me at any time. I kept myself in good spirits by playing positive, uplifting music. I also made sure that any equipment I needed for her care was to hand, so I wouldn't have to make lots of trips upstairs.

More than at any time in my life, I needed the support of my family and friends, and I am grateful for the support they gave me.

5.2: General advice

The following advice about recovery comes mainly from desktop research and the experiences of other mothers. We found **www.parents.com** and **www.familydoctor.org** especially useful.

1. Be prepared: in terms of recovery, 'normal' is relative. Recovery is generally expected to take six to eight weeks for vaginal birth and up to twelve weeks for Caesarean sections, but it could take much longer depending on the person. Prepare for your recovery by planning in advance and by eating, sleeping and resting well.

2. Know what's to come: postpartum, you should expect some bruising, swelling and nipple soreness. You will experience mild cramps (called afterpains) as a result of your contractions, hormonal changes, sweating during the night, and you may even experience some hair loss. Another common experience is urinary incontinence, especially when you laugh or cough too hard. It's best to wear pantyliners to maintain your personal hygiene during this period.

3. Stitches: you may have had stitches after giving birth, for example, as a result of tearing, if the doctor needed to make an incision or if you had a Caesarean section. It is imperative to keep the stitches clean to avoid secondary infection. If you had a Caesarean section, use the hospital-issued underwear or underwear without an elastic waistband to avoid irritating the stitches. A traditional (African) hot water press or pressing a hot water bottle against your lower abdomen and any sore areas can help the healing process and firm up stretched muscles.

4. Bleeding and spotting: it is very normal to experience heavy bleeding for up to two weeks after childbirth, and spotting could continue for up to six weeks or more. This bleeding, called lochia, often comes from where the placenta was detached after birth. There may occasionally be clots in the blood, but they should be small (usually smaller than 3cm in diameter). Mothers are advised to wear high-waisted mesh underwear during this period as this is strong enough to hold heavy soaked pads. Tampons are not recommended until you are fully recovered to avoid the risk of infection. If bleeding continues for too long, or if the clots are heavy, consult your doctor. The general rule is that if you feel something is wrong, it probably is.

5. Lifting and exercise: don't jeopardise your recovery by taking on too much too soon. You have been bored and are now recovering, and there is a temptation to immediately do more. Avoid this temptation at all costs! It is best to delay exercising again until your doctor says so and to avoid using stairs and lifting heavy objects. The general advice is to only lift items that weigh less than your baby.

6. Water retention and weight loss: for most new mothers, a key concern is to get rid of the extra weight and to return to their pre-pregnancy body shape and confidence. On average, mothers are likely to lose between seven and nine kilograms after the birth, with the remainder lost gradually over the coming months. It's best to be prepared to lose this extra weight gradually, rather than by following an aggressive programme that could be detrimental to your health.

7. Other health concerns: unfortunately, just making it past childbirth is not enough. Mothers continue to be exposed to postnatal health concerns and need to be vigilant about their health. In particular, watch for the following:

    a. Deep vein thrombosis (DVT): blood clots can form in the deep veins which can travel to the lungs and become fatal, and this can happen well after birth. Signs include leg pains or the feeling of pulling a muscle. Mothers are issued with tight stockings during childbirth and are encouraged to wear them for a while after birth to aid blood circulation.

    b. Haemorrhoids, or piles: these result from the swelling of the veins due to the strain of pushing during childbirth. Haemorrhoids will bleed, are painful and itchy. They usually shrink over time, but if not, consult your doctor.

    c. Postnatal pre-eclampsia: although this concern can arise anytime from during your pregnancy until after the birth, it is of particular concern during the postpartum period because mothers tend to think that the danger is over. Pre-eclampsia is the constriction of the veins which can lead to high blood pressure with potentially fatal consequences. It is evidenced by headaches, swelling of the feet and blurred vision among other symptoms. Consult your doctor immediately if you have these concerns.

Part IV

FROM BABY TO TODDLER

CHAPTER 6

The Toddler

What is a toddler and how is a toddler different from a baby or a child?

A toddler is a child that is just beginning to walk. The term comes from the word 'toddling', which means to walk around in an unsteady manner. So, where we often consider a child from birth to 12 months to be a baby, we generally consider a child to be a toddler when they are between the ages of 12 and 36 months.

While a toddler is defined by their ability to walk, as you may have already guessed, walking is not the first activity that a child will independently engage in. Children go through many milestones and growth stages. Here, we will look at a few of the early stages that babies and their parents reach, as well as some of the key experiences to look out for.

6.1: Weaning your baby

A baby is weaned off their mother when they have ceased to breastfeed and begin to derive their nutrition from other food sources. Although this term can also be used for withdrawing the baby's source of nutrition from the bottle, it is primarily associated with breast-feeding.

The schedule for weaning will differ from one society to another. While most experts in the West recommend that a baby should be breast-fed for a minimum of 12 months, it is not uncommon to see babies nurse for up to 24 months in other cultures.

Tip: For good growth, WHO recommends that a baby should be breast-fed exclusively for a minimum of six months. Six months is also considered the absolute minimum for other practical reasons, such as a mother's return to work.

An early indication that a baby is ready to start weaning is the development of their first set of teeth (the upper incisors). These teeth are very sharp and can deliver painful cuts to the mother's breast and nipple: a timely cue to begin the weaning process. For what foods to wean the baby onto, refer to Section 3.3.

As with many things, weaning is likely to involve withdrawal pains for the baby (and sometimes the mother) because breast-feeding not only serves nutritional purposes, but provides a very good means of connection between mother and child, and is a great source of comfort for the baby. In fact, this connection is so important that some cultures have weaning ceremonies.

6.2: Teething

As the name suggests, teething is the period in which your baby begins to develop their first set of teeth. Typically, teething occurs between the ages of four to seven months, but as always with babies, the timings can vary. This can be a rather painful period for your baby, and the symptoms can start months before the first tooth even appears.

Our daughter had developed swollen and itchy gums, and she kept chewing on her toys in an attempt to scratch them. The problem here was that her toys could have been infected with germs, which could lead to secondary issues. It is also common to see babies stooling during this period as a result of putting different things in their mouths to soothe their itchy gums.

Some other symptoms of teething include:

- Increased biting, for example, biting their mother's breasts, spoons, toys, clothes etc.
- Excessive drooling
- Disturbed sleeping patterns
- Fever, rashes, coughing and diarrhoea
- Pulling their ears and rubbing their chins to ease the pain
- Reduced appetite
- General irritability
- Visible signs of teeth growing below the gum

Note: Diarrhoea can be very serious for a baby. If your baby is stooling for over 24 hours, don't assume it is a teething symptom. Go and see your paediatrician.

There is a whole raft of remedies to help soothe your teething baby, and as always, it is best to seek professional advice. For our daughter, we used the same method as our parents: the world-famous Ashton &

Parsons® teething powder. Chances are, however, that you will not find this prescription in your local stores given that large pharmaceutical companies are focusing on more profitable brands. In our case, we had to order over the internet therefore I recommend that you ask your pharmacist or paediatrician for a suitable alternative.

Figure 6-1:

A popular brand of teething powder

6.3: Sitting up

The very first independent action that your baby will perform will be to attempt to lift their head and roll over. However, the first milestone that most parents really get excited about is when their baby begins sitting up on their own. Between the ages of four and eight months, many babies will attempt to sit up, pick up their dummy, put it in their mouth and then bask in this great accomplishment. They'll likely do so until they are capable of sitting up without any assistance.

To encourage our daughter to sit up, we often seated her on the floor supported with a U-shaped breast-feeding pillow. We found that this gave her the confidence to try sitting on her own. She would make several attempts until she succeeded, fell over and started again.

6.4: Crawling

After sitting, the next natural step is for your baby to begin crawling. This is another big event in the calendar of doting parents. Children tend to start crawling almost as soon as they learn to sit up; in fact, some children do both simultaneously. This usually takes place between the ages of six and 10 months, but do not be surprised if your baby skips the crawling phase altogether.

We put our daughter on a carpeted floor, supported her sitting position with the U-shaped pillow and placed a toy, such as a rattle, a few feet away. We would shake the rattle and encourage her to come and get it. I also recall my daughter crawling up the stairs of our two-storey home one evening in 2012 while the entire family videoed the event on their phones. She managed to climb all the way to the top, which gave us all a lot of joy. It must have been a challenging feat for her, though, because she never attempted it again!

The most important point here is, however you get your child to sit up or crawl, you must encourage and help your baby make these first few steps in life.

Tip: Once your baby begins to crawl, it is time to clear your house of all sharp and dangerous items. This includes sharp edges on pieces of furniture and books on lower shelves of bookcases, which can be easily retrieved and torn up.

6.5: Standing

Now your baby is on the move, you need to be on your guard: there is a great chance of the baby crawling towards danger. As a toddler, my younger sister crawled towards a pressing iron and burnt her hand. She still bears that mark almost 40 years later!

I consider crawling to be the stage in which your baby really begins to explore the world around them, and their natural tendency is to pull themselves up to stand upright, using anything from bookshelves to chairs or other items of furniture. Babies are expected to be able to stand between the ages of nine and 12 months, however some might not start walking for as long as 18 months.

As with many things, some babies simply do some things more quickly than others. Don't panic if your baby doesn't progress as quickly as you expect, but do seek professional advice.

Tip: Some think that it's best for babies to start walking later, as this gives their bones more time to strengthen and so reduces the risk of deformity from putting pressure on the legs too early. However, there is no empirical evidence to support this.

You may be surprised to find that your baby will stand but does not know how to sit back down. I watched our daughter do this and was baffled! This can be incredibly frustrating for babies as they are likely tired from standing. This is yet another stage in their development, and you will need to teach your baby to bend their knees. They may resist at first, but they will generally pick it up after a few days.

6.6: Walking

Once your baby is upright, their next natural step will be to try walking. Just like the transition from sitting to crawling, your baby may need encouragement to take their first steps. It is common to see babies stand up against a piece of furniture and pull themselves along. As soon as they start to feel confident, the baby is likely to attempt a few steps, or to 'toddle'. To start with, this toddling will not last long before they sit back down or fall over.

Walking can be expected as early as the 14th month but can start as late as the 20th month. Some toddlers are braver than others and will want to charge off alone, but it is recommended to hold their hand and gently pull them along as they take their first steps. You can also use a walker which a baby can lean on and push around, though some experts think this may not give the baby enough time to develop the strength they need in their legs. However, again, there are no hard and fast rules: most babies will learn to walk as long as you are there to provide the support they need.

Interestingly, I recall a combined baby seat and walker in the 1980–90s. It was round and could move in all directions, enabling the baby to walk and sit intermittently. This kind of device is no longer common, but it was a good design and bargain hunters can still find a few around.

There is plenty of good information online about how to help your baby as they start to walk. I'd recommend related articles on the website, www.babycentre.com.

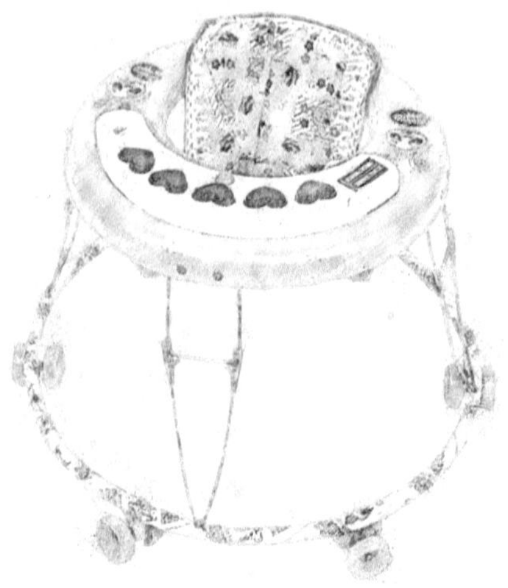

Figure 6-2:
A combined walker/bouncer

6.7: Talking

Hands up if you cried when your baby said their first word! Many parents are sentimental, and rightly so. Though I must confess that I missed my daughter's first words; I just picked up at some point that we could communicate.

Talking is the last of the many early milestones we wanted to cover here. Suffice it to say that your baby will not communicate in full sentences at first. Most babies start with the words 'mama' and 'dada', or 'no' – usually in relation to food – and 'boo'. My daughter said 'dada' first, which didn't sit too well with my wife considering that she did most of the parental 'heavy lifting' and was the primary caregiver. What can I say? It is an unfair world!

As with other baby milestones, the age at which a baby starts to speak varies, but it is typically expected to happen between the ages of 12 and 18 months. Babies may start to talk late, and it's possible that this is a signal of other developmental issues. You should consult a professional if you have concerns.

Tip: Experts have said that some children diagnosed with autism or ADHD were late talkers. If you're concerned about your baby's talking, see your paediatrician to address your concerns early.

CHAPTER 7

Meet the World

This section of the book is about the child's early schooling and meeting the world. The decision to send our daughter to early school was one of the more difficult decisions we took in her first three years. At the time, we lived in a village of less than 500 people in southern parts of the United Kingdom and our decision to send her to school had a lot to do with our location.

Firstly, we had limited options for jobs or for schooling in these rural parts. There are also fewer people and therefore fewer baby friends for our daughter. The decision to send her to early school was mainly driven by the need for her to develop good social skills from an early age by interacting with other toddlers. The second driver was the need to prepare her mother for her eventual return to work.

Like every decision that one makes, there are implications to this decision and the objective of this section is to assist the reader make as practical a decision as possible.

7.1: On early-year schooling

At some point between the ages of two and three, most new parents are likely to be asking themselves when is best to send their child to nursery or to leave their child with other carers. This is a rather difficult question to answer as it raises several issues, each of which is discussed here.

Firstly, there is the question of a second stage of 'weaning', as this may be the first time your child's primary care has been transferred to someone else. Secondly, there is the child's own development as the child might not be developed enough for nursery or childcare given that children develop at different speeds: some are early starters, while others are slower developers.

There is also the question of cost: nurseries, crèches and playgroups are not cheap anywhere in the world. In some countries, parents typically pay more for their child to attend a nursery than they will pay for their child to attend university because caring for babies and little children require a specific skill set and certain temperament. This issue is often compounded by the fact that the primary caregiver – usually the mother – has been out of work for a relatively long time, which will also impact the family's finances. It is not unusual for families to perform a cost–benefit analysis before sending their child to a nursery: is it worth paying a nursery more than the primary caregiver would earn on their return to work? For example, if a full-time nursery place for your child would cost £1,500 per month and you earn £1,800 a month after tax, you may decide that it isn't worth sending your child to nursery at all.

Then there is the question of the adequacy of the establishment:

- How clean is the nursery?
- Does it have the correct facilities?
- Do the staff have the necessary skills and training to look after the children?
- What is the ratio of staff to children?

Another issue is that of societal pressure. There was mild outrage, for example, when the French minister Rachida Dati returned to work just five days after having her baby in 2009. Society was not just concerned about whether she had made adequate provision for the care of the baby while she was away. Parents who are seen as sending their baby to nursery too early may be considered uncaring or unattached. Although, it is worth noting that the decisions for our child's care should not be driven by what others think, that pressure does exists, and it is more prevalent in certain cultures than others.

Finally, there is the emotional question of how quickly a mother can disengage from her baby and return to work. I was sad when I finally returned to work. I had developed a good routine with my daughter, making a breakfast, preparing her for the day, the midday naps and just watching her play around the room we shared together for most of the day. All this is incompatible with the daily grind of commuting and getting back to work after an extended absence, as I had taken an extended break after her birth, and I found myself thinking about her after she left for early school. Overall, I found that there isn't always a 'right' time to send your child to their first school or day-care, it is one of those decisions you take and live with the outfall off.

7.2: Guidance on selecting early schooling

For most educational systems, the first level of primary education (grade 1 or primary 1) begins at six years old, while a two-year pre-primary stage (such as nursery or playgroup) is generally the norm. Based on this, the typical age for starting formal schooling can be considered to be four years old.

However, most professional working parents will agree that taking a four-year career break would have a significant impact on their career – assuming you could find an employer who would accommodate such a break in the first place - some form of childcare is therefore a necessity for many working parents in the intervening years up to age four.

We first sent our daughter to nursery when she was 14 months old, and I know families who have sent their children even younger. While I won't make any recommendations in terms of the appropriate age, when you do decide the time is right, the list below will help you choose the right place.

1. Level of development: most early-years establishments have requirements relating to the level of development of the children that they will accept. Many early schools insist that the child should at least be able to stand and/or walk so they have at least some independence.

2. Full-time or part-time: having been nursed consistently by their primary caregiver up to this point, it can be challenging for the child (and also for the primary caregiver) to go straight into full-time hours at school or nursery. Instead, you may want to start with a part-time arrangement, such as half-days or alternate

days to start with to allow for a gradual settling in for all parties concerned.

3. Length of the school day: as you can expect, most nurseries and playgroups do not operate for the full length of the working day (i.e. from 9am to 5pm), but often close between midday and 2pm. This can create a commuting challenge for working parents, so it's important to consider what is best for your child. Do you want a nursery close to your work – taking into account your child's drop-off and pick-up times – or close to your home for convenience?

4. School rating: it is always good to check the school inspection's report for the school in which you are going to place your child. In the United Kingdom, for example, Ofsted ratings are available for schools on a rating from 1–4, where 1 is outstanding and 4 is inadequate.

5. Similar rankings are available from the educational regulators in many countries and should be a key criterion when selecting a school for your child.

6. Childcare facilities: an evaluation of what constitutes a 'good facility' will vary from parent to parent as it is an issue of personal preference, but I would encourage every parent to visit the nursery in person to see what is available and check the layout. Safety concerns should be paramount in your mind. I recall visiting a nursery in southeast England where the childcare unit was on the second floor, which we thought was an additional safety risk in the event of an evacuation. We also checked things such as fire exits, alarm systems and access control amongst other issues.

7. Staff to pupil ratio: another critical item of consideration is the staff to pupil ratio. Whereas a pupil to teacher ratio of between 15:1 or 25:1 is acceptable for primary schools, the ratio for nurseries is around three to five pupils for every adult, and any nursery with larger ratios should be avoided. You should also look out for the presence of teaching assistants, who support the teachers, and enquire about the experience of the teachers. It is a difficult job with a high attrition rate, but you don't want to commit the care of your child to someone who is just there to make money.

8. Class environment: I have already mentioned the importance of visiting the nursery before registering your child, and it'll come as no surprise that the most important area to visit is the actual class where the children will be spending most of their time.

   a. Is the area clear of hard or dangerous furniture?
   b. What kind of toys are available? For younger children, soft toys are best
   c. Do they have quiet areas for the children to take a nap? (Shocking as it may be, some nurseries for children under the age of three do not have resting areas!)
   d. Does the area have good lighting and cross ventilation?

9. Playground: for toddlers, the playground is the centre of their world. Here they play, socialise and become familiar with the concept of being outdoors. Most nurseries tend to have playgrounds, but it is worth doing a quick inspection all the same.

a. Is there direct access from the classroom to the playground?
b. Is the play equipment suitable for your child's age? If not, what are the alternatives?
c. Is the area secure and free from hazards?
d. Is there direct access from the playground to the street?

10. Medical support services: it is also worth checking the medical support available at the nursery, the procedures in place to contact parents in emergencies and the nursery's proximity to an adequate provider of secondary health services. It is a given that, being exposed to the outside environment and far from the safety of their homes, children in nurseries are likely to catch bugs or other minor illnesses. The nursery should have a procedure for administering first-response treatment, as well as an evacuation plan for more serious concerns, and parents should be kept informed at every point.

11. Food and hygiene: to ensure adequate hygiene, some parents prefer to pack lunches for their children, but even this is not foolproof, especially if the area where your child will be eating is not clean. If you opt for the food provided by the nursery, it is important to see the kitchen, how the food is served, where the children will have meals and to understand the type of assistance that staff can provide. You'll also want to ensure that the meals provide a balanced diet and that they are appealing to your child: there is no point having a healthy meal of spinach and cucumber on the menu when you know your child would never touch their greens! Compromise and common sense are required to get the right balance here.

12. Baby changing: some nurseries will insist that children are potty trained before they can be registered, however most will admit children from the age of 18 months and acknowledge that nappy changing comes with the territory. Although some ask that you provide a specified number of nappies each day, the more forward-looking ones offer to provide nappies as part of the fee. It is important to speak to the nursery about this service to confirm which member of staff will perform the change and how it will be supervised – particularly in the interest of safeguarding the child. As the child's clothes may need to be changed if soiled, make sure the nursery can provide a pre-wash service.

13. The curriculum: while sending children to nursery is not quite the same as sending them to school, some basic cognitive work takes place at this stage, so you'll want to ask about the curriculum. Below is an example of what my daughter covered at playgroup at the age of 14–17 months.

    a. Playing outside
    b. Playing in the push cars
    c. Walking around in the garden
    d. Musical merry-go-rounds
    e. Using pop-up toys
    f. Painting and dabbing
    g. Chalking and colouring
    h. Crafts
    i. Nursery rhymes
    j. Sleeping

This checklist is by no means exhaustive but is rather a reminder of some of the things to look out for as you visit the nurseries.

Tip: Before visiting a nursery for the first time, make a list of questions you want answered and things you want to see so that you can make the most of the visit.

Part V
EPILOGUE

CHAPTER 8

Advice From Other Mothers

Given the variety of opinions that any discussion on the subject of parenting generates, it would be short-sighted to limit the contents of this book to our experience alone. To this end, we surveyed a group of 30 mothers with the aim of getting a wider picture of birthing and postnatal experiences. Our sample population has been drawn across several cultures with respondents from the United Kingdom, the United States, Nigeria, Qatar, Canada and South Korea. Their responses are related to their experience with motherhood in general; the respondents are not necessarily first-time mothers but their responses were general enough to cover postnatal experiences.

We developed a simple, semi-structured questionnaire of 10 questions on issues ranging from birthing methods to childcare selection criteria. Their responses are summarised below.

It seems that the greatest fear for most mothers is miscarriage. This is understandable, as it is said that there is a greater risk of miscarriage for first-time mothers (although there are no studies to support this). Indeed, **www.tommys.org** suggest that up to 25% of pregnancies (1 in 4) end in miscarriage. Most of these miscarriages occur in the first trimester, with estimates ranging from 80–85% for miscarriages occurring in this period.

For women who do miscarry, it has been shown that it takes longer to conceive again, and that there is up to a 15% chance of suffering a second miscarriage. The good news, however, is that miscarriage does not decrease the likelihood of having a normal pregnancy next time round. For more information on miscarriages, visit **tommys' website**, or better still, speak to your gynaecologist.

A second finding was the preferred method for childbirth. Most women I know have had a Caesarean section, and I expected that the survey would highlight its widespread usage as a preference of mothers. However, our survey revealed that most mothers prefer natural births, the second most popular option is birth pools and the use of Caesarean sections was a distant third.

In response to the question of the greatest challenge that mothers faced after childbirth, the survey showed that the greatest challenge had to do with feeding – breast-feeding in particular. The challenges ranged from the inability of the mother to lactate to knowing when the baby has had enough. As mentioned, we faced similar difficulties when our daughter couldn't latch on. Sometimes the baby is willing to latch on, but the mother is not able to lactate. In such cases, it is possible to have a wet nurse, but do speak to your paediatrician about this.

Another common issue with breast-feeding is that some mothers feel vulnerable and uncomfortable feeding their babies in public. The United Kingdom in particular has been described as having one of the lowest levels of breast-feeding in the world, with only 34% of babies being breast-fed up to the age of six months. This is linked to the fact that public breast-feeding has been seen as controversial. However, there are many ways to feel more comfortable breast-feeding in public, such as using a scarf or shawl.

Figure 8-1: Breast-feeding with a shawl/scarf

It is worth highlighting another common theme in this category. Several respondents mentioned being confused by the plethora of advice they received from all and sundry. This can certainly be overwhelming, as parents need to filter out sound advice from old wives' tales. Having a confidant, such as your partner, a parent or close relative, who can shield you as well as act as a sounding board will help you eliminate unnecessary advice.

Another critical learning from the survey relates to the question of how soon to send a child to some form of childcare facility. All respondents confirmed that they sent their child to nursery before the age of four, with a significant proportion (62.5%) confirming that registration took place before the age of two years. The key thing to take away from this is that you shouldn't feel guilty about sending your child to nursery early; it is a sign of the changing society that we live in. Given the fact that our respondents were drawn from across six countries and four continents, this also indicated that some practices are becoming homogenous across cultures.

In terms of the selection of childcare, the survey showed that the most important factor was the available facilities. This was more important than cost, proximity or brand name.

Mothers also confirmed that their greatest desire immediately after childbirth was to have more help with activities such as household chores. Almost two out of three respondents suggested that they did not receive adequate assistance from their spouse or other members of the household with chores including cooking, cleaning and childcare. This should be a signal to partners and other close family members to take the load of household chores off new mothers.

The other significant area where mothers indicated that they needed assistance was emotional support. Hormonal issues must, of course, be addressed by health professionals, but even the overwhelming responsibility of caring for the child all day when others go to work can make the primary caregiver feel vulnerable. In such cases, partners and other family members can help by taking some time off to support the mother and look after the baby so that she has the opportunity to go out or even just have a moment to herself. Such small gestures may go a long way to aid and support her emotional wellbeing.

Finally, we asked mothers for the best advice that they had received and what they would pass on to mothers-to-be. These were the top three responses:

1. Enjoy the birth and childcare process, even the painful and difficult parts of it
2. Prepare mentally, spiritually and emotionally for this life-changing experience
3. Seek help whenever required, particularly professional help if you sense any psychological issues.

CHAPTER 9

Quotes and Daily Motivations

Here is some food for thought: it is important to remember that there will be many days when you will not feel up to the responsibility of caring for your child. There will be days when you will need someone to talk to, but they've gone to work. For such days, I present to you a list of learnings, quotes and words of wisdom that I garnered during those nursing days. They are not all specifically related to parenting, but they are all worth reflecting upon.

◇◇◇◇◇◇◇◇◇◇◇◇◇◇◇◇◇◇◇

 # 1

You cannot meet a target you did not set.

◇◇◇◇◇◇◇◇◇◇◇◇◇◇◇◇◇◇◇

 # 2

Learn to move forward every day. Nobody makes it in life by living in the past.

◇◇◇◇◇◇◇◇◇◇◇◇◇◇◇◇◇◇◇

3

There is nothing in your past that it is worth sacrificing your future for. Focus on your future, it is your focus that will become your reality.

4

Some things in life are invaluable, like family and friends. On their deathbed, nobody says 'I wish I made more money'. They always wish they had made the best of their opportunities and spent more time with their family.

5

Always have the hope that good will triumph over evil.

6

Sometimes we focus so much on the issues or challenges of life that we lose focus on our destination. Don't focus on your affliction and lose sight of your promise.

7

Every family should have one thing they agree on: one central value, one hope, one purpose and one direction.

◇◇◇◇◇◇◇◇◇◇◇◇◇◇◇◇◇◇◇

8

Often, we are too overwhelmed by problems that we refuse to see them as opportunities. All present-day billionaires solved a unique human problem; what are you doing for society?

◇◇◇◇◇◇◇◇◇◇◇◇◇◇◇◇◇◇◇

9

Let the unity of your home be a likeness of the unity of heaven.

◇◇◇◇◇◇◇◇◇◇◇◇◇◇◇◇◇◇◇

10

Marriages are the cornerstone of society because marriages are the basis of family and families are the basis of society.

◇◇◇◇◇◇◇◇◇◇◇◇◇◇◇◇◇◇◇

11

The key to success in life is managing your time. Anyone who controls your time controls your life.

◇◇◇◇◇◇◇◇◇◇◇◇◇◇◇◇◇◇◇

12

Bitter people usually end up alone in life.

◇◇◇◇◇◇◇◇◇◇◇◇◇◇◇◇◇◇◇

13

Scripture says 'train a child', not 'train a teenager'. The earlier you start training your child, the higher your chances of success.

◇◇◇◇◇◇◇◇◇◇◇◇◇◇◇◇◇◇◇

14

Greatness comes through service. Your life ambition must be greater than a big house and a nice car.

◇◇◇◇◇◇◇◇◇◇◇◇◇◇◇◇◇◇◇

15

The greatest gift that God has given us is other people and relationships.

 # 16

Passion is central to success in life: passionate people treat their work as their life, not as jobs.

 # 17

Life is about perspective. Do not give up on what God has given you simply because it is difficult to achieve.

 # 18

You need to be vulnerable. If you can't sacrifice your current life, you can't get a better life.

 # 19

Do what is right, but remember that what is right is often the opposite of what is popular.

 # 20

Yield to others. Success is not achieved by trampling on those around us.

 # 21

God has HIS prerogative on whom HE would use to bless you; it may even be through your enemy.

◇◇◇◇◇◇◇◇◇◇◇◇◇◇◇◇◇◇◇◇

 # 22

Tame your tongue. You don't have to have the last word in every argument.

◇◇◇◇◇◇◇◇◇◇◇◇◇◇◇◇◇◇◇

 # 23

Nothing can offend you without your permission. Avoid listening to what you find offensive and keep your fences up.

◇◇◇◇◇◇◇◇◇◇◇◇◇◇◇◇◇◇◇

 # 24

It is not enough to have a dream or desire; you must also have the right environment in which to nurture it and dream on a scale that pushes you.

◇◇◇◇◇◇◇◇◇◇◇◇◇◇◇◇◇◇◇

 # 25

If you need a change in life, you are the one to make it happen.

◇◇◇◇◇◇◇◇◇◇◇◇◇◇◇◇◇◇◇

 # 26

You will never change what you tolerate. Don't tolerate defeatism and mediocrity.

◇◇◇◇◇◇◇◇◇◇◇◇◇◇◇◇◇◇◇

 # 27

An opportunity of a lifetime must be taken during the lifetime of that opportunity. You need to pursue a dream in order to achieve it.

◇◇◇◇◇◇◇◇◇◇◇◇◇◇◇◇◇◇◇

 # 28

The storms of life are a certainty. Build for strength, for principle and moral clarity. Things built for strength are eternal; things built for beauty are temporary.

◇◇◇◇◇◇◇◇◇◇◇◇◇◇◇◇◇◇◇◇

 # 29

Don't let your circumstances or what you can see talk you out of what you have heard in your spirit.

◇◇◇◇◇◇◇◇◇◇◇◇◇◇◇◇◇◇◇◇

 # 30

Urgent things are not necessarily important things. Prioritise your own decisions. It is noble to get things done but more noble to know what you should ignore.

◇◇◇◇◇◇◇◇◇◇◇◇◇◇◇◇◇◇◇◇

 # 31

You will be hurt many times in life. Accept the accidental hurts, but remember that forgiveness is meant for the intentional hurts.

◇◇◇◇◇◇◇◇◇◇◇◇◇◇◇◇◇◇◇◇

 # 32

If you must birth something, there is often a process and a pain associated with it. Do not circumvent the process; the joy of achievement comes from this experience.

◇◇◇◇◇◇◇◇◇◇◇◇◇◇◇◇◇◇◇◇

 # 33

Do not let your environment dictate your character. People can ruin your reputation, but they cannot ruin your character.

◇◇◇◇◇◇◇◇◇◇◇◇◇◇◇◇◇◇◇◇

 # 34

There are two tests of character: prosperity and adversity. Handling adversity is typical, but can your character handle the test of prosperity?

◇◇◇◇◇◇◇◇◇◇◇◇◇◇◇◇◇◇◇

 # 35

Turn your power (financial, academic, social, etc.) to influence. Power that is not turned to influence wanes, but if power is turned to influence, both power and influence grow.

◇◇◇◇◇◇◇◇◇◇◇◇◇◇◇◇◇◇◇

 # 36

Understand your purpose. Purpose gives direction to your goals. Without purpose, the achievement of your goals simply amounts to small and hollow victories.

◇◇◇◇◇◇◇◇◇◇◇◇◇◇◇◇◇◇◇

 # 37

If you want to encourage a particular value in your home or family, you must reward the expression of that value. Only rewarded values are perpetuated.

◇◇◇◇◇◇◇◇◇◇◇◇◇◇◇◇◇◇◇

 # 38

The world will teach you about your rights. Choose to focus on your responsibilities.

◇◇◇◇◇◇◇◇◇◇◇◇◇◇◇◇◇◇◇

 # 39

Accept yourself and your personal flaws. Like dimples on a golf ball, your flaws will only make you go further.

◇◇◇◇◇◇◇◇◇◇◇◇◇◇◇◇◇◇◇

 # 40

I do not know the secret of success, but the secret of failure is trying to please everyone.

www.ingramcontent.com/pod-product-compliance
Ingram Content Group UK Ltd.
Pitfield, Milton Keynes, MK11 3LW, UK
UKHW040027200726
13854UKWH00001B/397